First World War
and Army of Occupation
War Diary
France, Belgium and Germany

59 DIVISION
178 Infantry Brigade
Sherwood Foresters
(Nottinghamshire and Derbyshire Regiment)
2/7th Battalion
1 May 1916 - 31 January 1918

WO95/3025/6

The Naval & Military Press Ltd
www.nmarchive.com
Published in association with The National Archives

Published by

The Naval & Military Press Ltd

Unit 10 Ridgewood Industrial Park,

Uckfield, East Sussex,

TN22 5QE England

Tel: +44 (0) 1825 749494

www.naval-military-press.com

www.nmarchive.com

This diary has been reprinted in facsimile from the original. Any imperfections are inevitably reproduced and the quality may fall short of modern type and cartographic standards.

© **Crown Copyright**
Images reproduced by permission of The National Archives, London, England, 2015.

Contents

Document type	Place/Title	Date From	Date To
Heading	WO 3025 59th Div 178 Inf Bde 2-7th BN Notts & derby Regt Feb 1917-1918 Jan		
Heading	2-7th Bn Notts & Debby Regt Feb 1917-1918 Jan		
Heading	War Diary Of 2/7 (Robin Hood) Bn The Sherwood Foresters Nottinghamshire & Derbyshire Regiment From 2nd Feb 1917 To 28th Feb 1917 Volume 1.		
War Diary	Fovant	02/02/1917	02/02/1917
War Diary	Folkestone	03/02/1917	04/02/1917
War Diary	Boulogne	07/02/1917	07/02/1917
War Diary	Villers Bretonneux	08/02/1917	09/02/1917
War Diary	Morcourt	10/02/1917	10/02/1917
War Diary	Foucaucourt	11/02/1917	11/02/1917
War Diary	Fovant	13/02/1917	13/02/1917
War Diary	Trenches	19/02/1917	19/02/1917
War Diary	Fovant	25/02/1917	27/02/1917
War Diary	Foucaucourt	26/02/1917	26/02/1917
War Diary	Southampton	26/02/1917	26/02/1917
War Diary	Shorncliffe	27/02/1917	27/02/1917
War Diary	Havre	27/02/1917	27/02/1917
War Diary	Boulogne	28/02/1917	28/02/1917
War Diary	Saleux	28/02/1917	28/02/1917
War Diary	Havre	28/02/1917	28/02/1917
War Diary	Vers	01/03/1917	01/03/1917
War Diary	St Fuscien	02/03/1917	02/03/1917
War Diary	Warfusee	03/03/1917	09/03/1917
War Diary	Bois St. Martin	10/03/1917	23/03/1917
War Diary	Brie	24/03/1917	26/03/1917
War Diary	Bouvincourt	27/03/1917	28/03/1917
War Diary	Bernes	29/03/1917	31/03/1917
Miscellaneous	Operation Order By Lieut-Col. F. Rayner, D.S.O., Commanding 2/7th Bn. Sherwood Foresters	14/03/1917	14/03/1917
War Diary	Bernes	01/04/1917	01/04/1917
War Diary	Vendelles	02/04/1917	13/04/1917
War Diary	Roisel	14/04/1917	18/04/1917
War Diary	Templeux	19/04/1917	20/04/1917
War Diary	Roisel	21/04/1917	21/04/1917
War Diary	L3d1.6 (ur Templeux)	22/04/1917	30/04/1917
War Diary	Hargicourt	01/05/1916	01/05/1916
War Diary	Roisel	04/05/1917	04/05/1917
War Diary	Hargicourt	05/05/1917	07/05/1917
War Diary	Bernes	07/05/1917	29/05/1917
War Diary	Hamelet	30/05/1917	30/05/1917
War Diary	Equancourt	31/05/1917	31/05/1917
War Diary	In The Field	01/06/1917	30/09/1917
Miscellaneous	Operation Orders By Lt Col M.C. Martyn M.C. Commanding 2/7th Sherwood Foresters	24/09/1917	24/09/1917
Miscellaneous	Operation Order By Lt Col M.C. Martyn M.C. Commanding 2/7th Sherwood Foresters	24/09/1917	24/09/1917
Map	Map B		
Miscellaneous	No.4 To Operation		

| Miscellaneous | 178th Infantry Brigade | 02/10/1917 | 02/10/1917 |
| War Diary | | 01/10/1917 | 31/01/1918 |

WO 3025
59th Div 17th INF Bde

2-7th Bn NOTTS + DERBY
Regt

Feb 1917 - 1918 Jan

59TH DIVISION
178TH INFY BDE

2-7TH BN NOTTS & DERBY REGT

FEB 1917 — ~~JLY 1918~~

1918 JAN

(ABSORBED by 7 BN)

Confidential.

WAR DIARY.

of

2/7 (Robin Hood) Bn. The Sherwood Foresters
Nottinghamshire & Derbyshire Regiment.

From 2nd Feb. 1917. to. 28th Feb. 1917.

Volume 1.

Army Form C. 2118.

WAR DIARY
or
INTELLIGENCE SUMMARY
(Erase heading not required.)

F. Raynor Lt Col.

Instructions regarding War Diaries and Intelligence Summaries are contained in F. S. Regs., Part II. and the Staff Manual respectively. Title Pages will be prepared in manuscript.

Place	Date	Hour	Summary of Events and Information	Remarks and references to Appendices
FOVANT.	2/2/17	11:30 pm	Instructional Advance party, consisting of 5 Officers & 14 N.C.O's & men.	1.
FOLKESTONE	3/2/17	6 am	Entrained at DINTON at 11:30 pm for FOLKESTONE. Arrived FOLKESTONE 6 am & spent night in Rest Camp.	
Do.	4/2/17	9:30 am	Embarked 9:30 am. Arrived BOULOGNE 12 noon. N.C.O's & men proceeded to OSTROHOVE Rest Camp, and officers to Hotels.	
BOULOGNE	7/2/17	11:30 pm	Entrained BOULOGNE at 11:30 pm for VILLERS BRETONNEUX.	
VILLERS BRETONNEUX	8/2/17	10 am	Arrived VILLERS BRETONNEUX 10 am & spent night in billets.	
"	9/2/17	5 pm	At 5 pm proceeded by Mechanical transport to MORCOURT & were attached to 1/4 EAST YORKS REGT.	
MORCOURT	10/2/17	10:30 am	Left MORCOURT at 9:30 am, arrived FOUCAUCOURT 2 pm & billeted for the night.	
FOUCAUCOURT	11/2/17	11:30 pm	Left billets 11:30 pm enroute for trenches.	
FOVANT	13/2/17		Captain R.A. CHARLTON and batman proceeded to HAVRE via SOUTHAMPTON for landing duties.	
TRENCHES	19/2/17	10 pm	Instructional advance party relieved at 10 pm by DURHAM LIGHT INFANTRY and returned to FOUCAUCOURT to billets.	

Army Form C. 2118.

WAR DIARY
or
INTELLIGENCE SUMMARY
(Erase heading not required.)

J Mayor Lt.Cl.

Instructions regarding War Diaries and Intelligence Summaries are contained in F. S. Regs., Part II. and the Staff Manual respectively. Title Pages will be prepared in manuscript.

Place	Date	Hour	Summary of Events and Information	Remarks and references to Appendices
FOVANT.	25/3/17	9.45 am	The Transport Advance Party, consisting of all the horses and Mule transport with suitable personnel, entrained at FOVANT railhead at 9/45 am proceeded to SOUTHAMPTON and entrained during afternoon.	
"	26/3/17		MAIN BODY entrained at railhead FOVANT as follows:- Letters B, C & D Companies at 11/40 pm	
"	27/3/17		Letter A Company at 1/45 am 27th.	
FOUCAUCOURT	26/3/17		Divisional Advance Party left FOUCAUCOURT & marched to WARFUSÉE and billeted there till arrival of main body.	
SOUTHAMPTON	"	7 am	Transport Advance Party sailed from SOUTHAMPTON at 7 am and anchored off NETLEY until 3 pm. Arrived off HAVRE at midnight.	
SHORNCLIFFE	27/3/17		Main Body detrained at SHORNCLIFFE and marched to rest billets at FOLKESTONE. At 9.30 am Embarked for Boulogne BOULOGNE. The night was spent in OSTROHOVE Rest Camp.	
HAVRE			Transport Advance Party's ships berthed at HAVRE at 2 am. Party disembarked and spent night in No. 2 Rest Camp Capt CHARLTON	
BOULOGNE	28/3/17		Main Body entrained for SALEUX as follows: A & B Coys. 3.45 am. C & D Coys. 8.55 am.	

Army Form C. 2118.

WAR DIARY
or
INTELLIGENCE SUMMARY
(Erase heading not required.)

F. Rayner L.A. 3

Place	Date	Hour	Summary of Events and Information	Remarks and references to Appendices
SALEUX	28/2/17		On arrival, the main body concentrated at VERS and billeted for the night	
HAVRE			8am Transport Advance party entrained 8am for LONGNEAU.	

WAR DIARY or INTELLIGENCE SUMMARY

Army Form C. 2118.

2/7 Sherwood Foresters
March 1917

No I

Place	Date	Hour	Summary of Events and Information	Remarks and references to Appendices
VERS	1/3/17		Main Body marched to ST FUSCIEN and billeted for the night. The Transport & Advance Party detrained at LONGNEAU and marched to ST. FUSCIEN where they joined the Main Body.	
ST. FUSCIEN	2/3/17		The Battalion marched to WARFUSÉE and was quartered in huts. The Instructional Advance Party joined the Battalion on this date.	
WARFUSÉE	3/3/17 to 8/3/17		Cleaning & improving the camp carried out by the Battalion. Training was continued.	
	9/3/17		The Battalion marched to BOIS ST. MARTIN [Ref ROSIÈRES Combined] and was quartered in huts. Sheet V. Wood. R.29.B.2.4.	
BOIS ST. MARTIN	10/3/17 to 14/3/17		Cleaning & improving the camp was carried out.	
	12/3/17	7/30 pm	Working party of 6 officers, 30 NCO's + 300 men paraded at 7/30 pm for work under supervision of R.E. at BERNY Dump	
	13/3/17	6/30 am	The above mentioned party returned to camp at 6/30 am.	
	15/3/17		The advance party for instructions on the trenches proceeded as per attached copy of orders.	
	16/3/17		The Battalion continued improving the camp. 5 working parties with following personnel were required by R.E.'s 5 Officers 249 O.R.	

WAR DIARY
INTELLIGENCE SUMMARY

Army Form C. 2118.

Place	Date	Hour	Summary of Events and Information	Remarks and references to Appendices
BOIS ST MARTIN	17/3/17		Improving Camp continued. 7 working parties with 9 officers and 354 O.R. were required by H.Q's.	
	18/3/17		The party attached to 2/4 Lincs. Regt. for instruction returned to camp at 6 p.m. Divine Service was held at 9 a.m. & Holy Communion was celebrated immediately after the service.	
	19/3/17		Improving the camp & Rifle Range [R17 b.2.2 (ROSIÈRES)] was continued. 7 working parties with 7 officers & 375 O.R. were required.	
	20/3/17	10/15 a.m.	The Battalion moved at 10/15 a.m. & relieved the 2/4 Lincs. Regt at BELLOY-EN-SANTERRE. The Quartermaster's Stores & Transport lines were established at ESTRÉES. [N25 d.5.5 (ROSIÈRES)]	
	21/3/17		Improving dug-out accommodation carried out. 5 Working parties were required with 5 officers & 340 O.R. for work on ESTRÉES-VILLERS-CARBONNEL Road.	
	22/3/17		The Battalion was employed on the road from BELLOY to main road ESTRÉES-VILLERS CARBONNEL [N27 d6.6.5 (ROSIÈRES)]. The Q.M. Stores & Transport moved to VILLERS-CARBONNEL.	
	23/3/17		The Battalion moved to BRIE and occupied trenches South of the BRIE-MONS-EN-CHAUSÉE road in O.33 and O.34 (French maps 62c S.W.) work was immediately commenced in organising the old German trenches into suitable trenches for the defence of the Bridgehead. ATHIES WOOD No. 1 (O35d) was organised for defence. The Battn. on our left was 2/5 N.& D. and that on our right 2/5 S. STAFFS.	

WAR DIARY or INTELLIGENCE SUMMARY

Place	Date	Hour	Summary of Events and Information	Remarks and references to Appendices
BRIE	24/3/17		Work continued as on 23rd.	
	25/3/17		do.	
	26/3/17		The Battn. moved to BOUVINCOURT (P23 c) Letter B Coy. proceeded to HANCOURT (Q8) and one strong platoon occupied the mine crater at K 33 a.8.4 (Ref b2c) Letter D Coy. commenced a diversion road round the mine crater at P30 d.1.6	
BOUVINCOURT	27/3/17		Battn continued the work at the mine crater commenced by Letter D Coy.	
	28/3/17		The Battn. moved to BERNES (Q4 c 8.1) as per attached operation orders & commenced constructing cruciform strong point at Q4.d.9.5, Q4.d.10, Q4 a 55.15 and Q3 c 25.55 in accordance with orders from 178th Infantry Bde.	
BERNES	29/3/17		Work Continued as Commenced on 28th.	
	30/3/17		do. 29th. 6 O.R. were wounded by artillery fire.	
	31/3/17		Work continued as on 30th. Lewis guns assisted the Sherwood Foresters in an attack on VENDELLES (R7) Carrying parties were also supplied.	

H.J. Nawson.
Maj.
Cmdg 2/7 Sherwood For.s.

SECRET.

OPERATION ORDER BY LIEUT.-COL.F.RAYNER, D.S.O.,   NO. 1.
COMMANDING 2/7TH BN. SHERWOOD FORESTERS.

14th March, 1917.

(1) The 178th Infantry Brigade will relieve the 177th Infantry Brigade on nights of 16/17th March and 17/18th March.

(2) The undermentioned details of the Battalion will be attached to the 4th Lincolns.Regt. (support battalion at BELLOY) for instruction :-
   (a) Commanding Officer.
       Adjutant.
       Bombing Officer.
       Intelligence Officer.
       Signalling Officer.
       One Officer per Company.) To be detailed
       One N.C.O. per platoon.   ) by Os.C.Companies.
       Three trained Signallers, and
       One Batman per Officer.
       This party will parade at 4 p.m. on the 15th March. Guides will meet them at the cross roads centre of ASSEVILLERS (M.13.b.7.6.) at 6/30 p.m.

   (b) Two runners to be detailed by Letters "A" & "C" Coys. They will report to O.C., No.4 Section, Divisional Signal Coy. at P.C. BICHAT (M.31.b.3.8.) at 5/30 p.m. to-day.

   (c) Carrying party. Two men per company will be detailed as carrying party. This party will report to H.Q., 2/5th Sherwood Foresters at M.27.c.3.2. at 4/30 p.m. on the 15th March.

   (d) Two D.R.Signallers will be detailed by the Signalling Officer to report to Brigade Headquarters (P.C.BICHAT) M.31.b.3.8., at 12 noon on the 14th March. This party will take with them the unconsumed portion of the day's ration and in addition the rations for two days.

   (e) Transport. The Transport Officer and the Transport Sergeant will report to the Transport Officer, 4th Lincolns, before 12 noon on 17th March (day before we relieve) at FOUCACOURT. Accommodation will be found for them by the T.O., 4th Lincolns.

(3) Guides will be in the proportion of two per platoon (or equivalent body of troops); one will lead in front and one follow behind.

(4) All ranks attached, except those mentioned in para.2 (d), will be rationed by the 4th Lincolns from the day after arrival inclusive.

(5) Dress - Fighting Order with greatcoats.

(6) Officers' spare baggage and men's packs and blankets will be carefully labelled and handed in to Q.M. Stores at least 2 hours before parades.

                                                F.PRAGNELL.
                                                Capt. & Adjt.

SECRET.

2/7 Sherwood Foresters.   **April 1917.**

Army Form C. 2118.

WAR DIARY or INTELLIGENCE SUMMARY

(Erase heading not required.)

Instructions regarding War Diaries and Intelligence Summaries are contained in F. S. Regs., Part II. and the Staff Manual respectively. Title Pages will be prepared in manuscript.

Place	Date	Hour	Summary of Events and Information	Remarks and references to Appendices
BERNES	April 1st		Wiring & improving strong posts continued during the day. At night the Batt. relieved 7/6 Sherwood Foresters in the trenches at VENDELLES. (R.1.c.)	
VENDELLES	2nd		The Battalion unsuccessfully attacked LE VERGUIER (L33.b) Casualties Capt. St George wounded & missing; Capt. Glascoyne wounded & missing; 2/Lt Downer (8th R. Manchester Regt attd 2/7 SF) missing believed killed. Other ranks 1 killed 15 wounded 11 missing. 9 wounded missing.	
	3rd		The Battn remained in the trenches at VENDELLES during the day. The Command of the Battn was temporarily taken over by Major M. Charlton M.C. of 2/8 Bn Sherwood Foresters. At night the 2/7 S.F. were relieved in trenches R.2.a & c. Strong posts at R.2.b were also taken over. A patrol consisting of Lieut C. C. Charlton & 16 O.R. proceeded to L.33.a in the trenches to ascertain if LE VERGUIER was occupied. 2/Lt Leggatt & 2/Lt Spencer were in charge of support patrols. Our stores moved forward to Q.19.d.9.4. Casualties NIL.	
	4th		Improving trenches & strong posts continued. Letters 'B' & 'C' Coys were placed at the disposal of O.C. 2/5 S.F. whilst attacking LE VERGUIER. 2/Lt Hatherall & 2/Lt S. Skelton & 12 N.C.Os reconnoitred the enemy wire about L.33. c & d.3 (?620). 2 Lewis gun teams were provided to cover a Coy. of 2/6 SF whilst digging a line of trenches at R.3.a.7.8. Casualties 2 OR wounded.	
	5th		Wiring & strong posts were continued. At night the following reliefs were accomplished. A Coy. 2/7 & occupied new strong posts at R.9.a.7.7. R.3.c.5.0, R.3.c.5.3, R.3.c.3.5. B Coy. took over strong posts from 2/6 S.F. at L.26.d and L.32.b.	

WAR DIARY or INTELLIGENCE SUMMARY

Army Form C. 2118.

Place	Date	Hour	Summary of Events and Information	Remarks and references to Appendices
VENDELLES	5th		Coy took over trenches from 2/6 S.F. at R.30 central. 2/ Coy took over strong post from 1/1 Oxford & Bucks L.I. at R.35.c.7.6, R.4.c.9.1, R.9.b.3.2. R.9.b.1.5. R.9.a.6.5. Observation post at R.9.a.8.8. Casualty 1 O.R. wounded 2nd reported.	
	6th		Trenches & strong posts improved. Letter B Coy handed over strong post at L.26.d. to 2/6 S. Stafford Regt. Casualties 1 O.R. wounded. 1 O.R. reported missing now reported wounded.	
	7th		Wiring & improvement of trenches. Casualties 2 O.R. killed 3 wounded	
	8th		Batt'n relieved in trenches in front of LE VERGUIER by 2/5 S.F. & returned to VENDELLES	
	9th		Cleaning up of village & filling in of craters between VENDELLES and BERNES.	
	10th		Battalion rested & at night carrying parties were supplied for 2/5 S.F. & LE VERGUIER.	
	11th		Battalion moved to ROISEL in billets on relief by 2/5 S. Staffords.	
	12th		Battalion rested & improved billets.	
	13th		Working parties of 6 Officers & 330 O.R. were supplied to 178th Inf. Bde.	

Army Form C. 2118.

WAR DIARY
or
INTELLIGENCE SUMMARY
(Erase heading not required.)

Instructions regarding War Diaries and Intelligence Summaries are contained in F. S. Regs., Part II. and the Staff Manual respectively. Title Pages will be prepared in manuscript.

Place	Date	Hour	Summary of Events and Information	Remarks and references to Appendices
ROISEL	Apr 14th		Inspection of Batn. by G.O.C. 179th Inf. Bde. cancelled owing to rain. Church Parade cancelled. Holy Communion 11.45 a.m. Afternoon observed as a holiday. Casualties Nil.	
	15th		Inspection of Batn. by G.O.C. 178th Inf. Bde. at 9.15 a.m. at K.22. d.7.8. Training under Coy. Commanders, practice of attack formations. Casualties Nil.	
	16th		Improvement of billets, cleaning up & repairing roads &c in ROISEL. Casualties Nil.	
	17th		Whole Batn. employed on working parties. 3 groups supplied as follows:- 20 groups on roads near HANCOURT. 5 Groups on roads near VRAIGNES. 8 " " " " HERVILLY. 2 Groups joining R.E. dumps at K.35. L.8.0 1 group loading stores at Q.8 c.8.4. 1 group loading stores at BERNES. Officers Staff Ride 1.45 p.m. Casualties Nil.	
	18th		1 Officer + 50 O.R. working at ROISEL crater K.17. a. 0.0 during the day. Casualties Nil.	
TEMPLEUX	19th		D Platoons of A Coy + all B Coy took over the front line between PILLERET and GRAND PRIEL WOODS from 13 Coy. N. Lincs Regt. Posts were held at L.11. a. 9.5. L.17. d. 4.7, L.11. d. 5.3, L.11. d. 3.1 + L.10. d. 4.8. Coy H.Q. were at L.16. b. 3.2. Batthn. H.Q. + remainder of Batthn. marched to TEMPLEUX LE GUERARD + took over from N. Lincs. Regt. Casualties Nil.	
	20th		Working party during the morning from D Coy improving roads + billets. Working party Royal Engineers. Working party at L.5.c. under Capt. Cooper	

TEMPLEUX

WAR DIARY or INTELLIGENCE SUMMARY

(Erase heading not required.)

Army Form C. 2118.

Place	Date April	Hour	Summary of Events and Information	Remarks and references to Appendices
TEMPLEUX	20th		Troops from C & D Coys during the night. B Coy & part of A Coy were relieved by 1/6 & 1/8 Bn. S.F. on reorganization of Brigade front and returned to ROISEL. Battn. returned to ROISEL from TEMPLEUX and went into Brigade reserve. Casualties 3 OR wounded.	
ROISEL	21st		Similar working parties to those of work in improving billets in ROISEL. 2/Lts were at work during the night. Casualties 2 OR slightly wounded.	
L3a16 (nr TEMPLEUX)	22nd		Battn. took over left battalion front from 1/6 S.F. Battn HQ moved from ROISEL to Quarry in L3d 1.6. A patrol under Lt Stokes entered the old German trench at L11a 9.5 and worked as far as the road at L5 d 3.6 without opposition. At barricade across the road 50 x W of the point L5 d 3.6 was occupied by an enemy sentry group. Shots were exchanged with the sentry group & one of the enemy was seen to be wounded. Rifle & machine gun fire was opened on the patrol from the Quarry and neighbourhood. The patrol returned safely. A patrol under 2/Lt Kimberley HCR reconnoitred the rifle pits in L5 b. These were seen to be occupied. 1 Off (slightly) & 2 OR wounded. Casualties. 3 OR killed. Work was continued in improving & wiring existing posts & advanced main lines. A patrol under 2/Lt W. Cook reconnoitred the egg shaped depression in L11 b. 200 x S of the Quarry & was found to be an flat guard unoccupied by the enemy. A patrol under Lt W. Cook reconnoitred	
	23rd			

WAR DIARY
or
INTELLIGENCE SUMMARY

Army Form C. 2118.

(Erase heading not required.)

Instructions regarding War Diaries and Intelligence Summaries are contained in F. S. Regs., Part II. and the Staff Manual respectively. Title Pages will be prepared in manuscript.

Place	Date	Hour	Summary of Events and Information	Remarks and references to Appendices
L3 d.1.6 nr TEMPLEUX	April 23rd		The line of rifle pits in L5.b. trench or line of rifle pits runs N.W. from the cross roads in L5.b. this was occupied by the Enemy. Casualties 4 O.R. wounded.	
	24th		Work was continued on our posts. 80 of new double apron were put up round our post at L4.b.0.6. A patrol under L/Sgt Shephard went along the road from L5.c.2.5 as far as the cross roads at L5.b.2.7. The enemy patrols were seen. HARICOURT was heavily shelled from 10/30 to 11/30 p.m. Casualties. Previously reported wounded 10.R. Killed 2.O.R. wounded 2 O.R.	
	25th	11/30 p.m.	A party of 3 offrs. 46 O.R. + 2 Lewis guns went out under Lieut W. Foster to occupy the quarry in F.29.c.8.5. The position was occupied without opposition at 2/30 am 26/4/17 and L/Sgt Shephard took charge of the post. Work was continued on our defences. An O.P. was constructed at L10.d.6.8. Casualties 2 O.R. wounded.	
	26th		The post in the quarry at F.29.c.8 was consolidated. It was heavily shelled during the day but no casualties occurred. Casualties killed 1 O.R. wounded 3 O.R.	
	27th		The 2/6 + 2/8 S.F. attacked the quarry in L5.d and COLOGNE FARM at dawn. The latter had to be abandoned later owing to shelling & machine gun fire. The quarry in L5.d and adjacent trenches remained in our hands. At right the post in the quarry at F.29.c.8 was taken over by the 48th Division.	

Army Form C. 2118.

2449 Wt. W14957/M90 750,000 1/16 J.B.C. & A. Forms/C.2118/12.

WAR DIARY
or
INTELLIGENCE SUMMARY

(Erase heading not required.)

Place	Date	Hour	Summary of Events and Information	Remarks and references to Appendices
13d.1.6 or TEMPLEUX	Apr 27th 28th		Mining was carried out in front of our posts at L10 d 5.3 and L4 b 7.5 Casualties: 1 OR killed, 3 OR wounded. The following took over the positions captured by the 1/6 & 2/8 S.F. in the attack of 27th. A Coy held from the egg shaped quarry in L11 b to the right edge of the quarry in L5 d: C Coy held the quarry with D Coy holding the captured trench from the quarry as far as L5 d 7.7. B Coy held their own posts and the advanced posts left by A Coy. 1/4 Coy of 1/4 Leic. was used to strengthen the front line. Casualties: 1 Officer killed, 3 OR wounded.	
	29th		The positions taken over were reorganised and consolidated. Our right Coy front was handed over to the 1/5 SF and the front reorganised as follows: A Coy from the quarry in L11 b inclusive to the quarry in L5 d exclusive. B & C Coy in the quarry and D Coy in same position on left flank. Casualties: 3 OR wounded. 2 OR wounded slightly, at duty.	
	30th		Our snipers were very successful on the left flank against the enemy in the trench round MALAKOFF FARM. Eight men were killed in this way,- they were shot as they tried to get away from the fire of our heavy artillery, who were wire-cutting in this area. Several enemy snipers were silenced and complete mastery obtained in this part of the front. Casualties: 2 OR killed 4 OR wounded	

M. McIntyre
Major
Commanding 2/7 Sherwood Foresters.

Army Form C. 2118.

2/7 Sherwood Foresters.

WAR DIARY
INTELLIGENCE SUMMARY
(Erase heading not required.)

May 1917.

Vol 4

Place	Date	Hour	Summary of Events and Information	Remarks and references to Appendices
HARGICOURT	1st May		Battalion was relieved in front line by 2/6 and 2/8 Sherwood Foresters and went into Brigade Reserve at ROISEL. Casualties 1 OR killed 5 OR wounded.	
ROISEL	4 May		Battalion received orders to man line of resistance and moved up at 11 p.m. Bn. Onward HQ moved to Quarry Q.3.d.3.7. Casualties 1 OR wounded	
HARGICOURT	5 May		Battn. moved into position N. of MALAKOFF FARM. Battn. forward HQ moved to Quarry in Q.10.a at 5 p.m. Attack cancelled 8.30 p.m. HQ went up into front line trenches at L.5.b. returning on May 7th.	
	6 May		Battn. was relieved by 2/6 N.Staffs Regt.	
	7 May		Latter Party returned from front line trenches at 4 a.m.	
BERNES	17/27 May		From 7th to 28th May inclusive, the Battn. was in reserve at the SUCRERIE, BERNES (Q.4.a) Training was carried out by Companies & Platoons every morning. Working parties (improvements to the camp and roads during the afternoon. Working parties were sent out nearly every night, principally for wiring and trench digging in front of LE VERGUIER and GRAND PRIEL WOOD. Working parties were also found during the day for road work under the Royal Engineers. Decoration: 2nd Lieut. W. Foster was awarded the Military Cross on 21st May.	
			Battn. moved to HAMELET and occupied the camp at K.20.b.2.0 for the night.	
HAMELET	29 May		Battn. marched from HAMELET to EQUANCOURT and occupied the camp at V.16 & Central for the night.	
EQUANCOURT	30 May		Battn. relieved 1/10 Bn. Manchester Regt. in the trenches in QSC during the night. Battn. HQ were at Q15.c.8.5. The relief was completed without incident.	
	31 May			

31st May / 1st June

M. W. Wyn
2nd Lt 2/7 Sherwood Foresters

2449 Wt. W14957/M90 750,000 1/16 J.B.C. & A. Forms/C.2118/12.

WAR DIARY or INTELLIGENCE SUMMARY

Army Form C. 2118.

178/59.

2/7 Shropshire Yeomanry Vol 5

5·X

Place	Date	Hour	Summary of Events and Information	Remarks and references to Appendices
In the Trenches	1917		Ref Sheet 57c SE	
	1st		Nothing of importance happened. A little shelling took place in neighborhood of Bilham Farm but no casualties were incurred.	
	2nd	12.50pm	Patrol of 2 Officers and 4 Other Ranks left our lines to reconnoitre ground in neighborhood of HOLLOW. The patrol got separated and party under 2/Lt Westbury met an enemy patrol. Shots were exchanged but one of our own was hit. Our Patrol detained. Hit on the enemy. Operations were carried out by us on the night of 2nd. Digging Posts in front of our Front line.	
	3rd		Digging was again resumed on the Posts without interruption. Battalion Head-quarters were shelled during the day.	
	4th 5th		Digging resumed on Potato Rifle at Q5d.3.7 and Q5d.9.5 Digging and Wiring of New Posts at Q5d.3.4 and Q5d.9.5. A little enemy rifle fire in front of Bilham Farm at 10pm. One hit was obtained. Killing 1 N.C.O. and 2 men	
	6th		Battalion was relieved by 4/5 Shropshire Yeomanry and went to NEUVILLE	
	7th-11th		P22d at Reserve Battalion. Working Parties were found.	
	11th 15th	4	Headquarters of A and B Coys moved from NEUVILLE & EQUANCOURT. V106-95 C and D Coys moved from NEUVILLE to EQUANCOURT. V106-95	
	11-20th		Battalion in Rest. Training carried out.	

Army Form C. 2118.

WAR DIARY
or
INTELLIGENCE SUMMARY
(Erase heading not required.)

2/7 Sherwood Foresters

Place	Date	Hour	Summary of Events and Information	Remarks and references to Appendices
In the Field	1917			
	12	9.	Battalion relieved 2/5 Sherwoods in front line trenches in front of BEAUCAMP.	
		9.12.6	Nothing of importance happened.	
	13	9.	A Patrol of ours came in touch with enemy in No Mans Land. Our Patrol waited until enemy were within 15 yds of them and then opened fire on them. Bombs were then first placed and finally Bayonet charge was made by us. We inflicted severe casualties to the enemy and all our men returned safely.	
	14	9.	Patrol went out to bring in German bodies left from previous encounter. Bodies had evidently been removed but German Rifle Bombs and M[ach]ine buttons were found.	
	25	9.14.9.50	Enemy Patrol tried to raid our Trenches but they were driven off leaving 3 dead in our hands. Otherwise enemy very quiet.	
	26	9.	Patrol went out to encounter enemy but they were not seen.	
	27	9.	Nothing of importance happened.	
	28	9.	A Patrol of 2 Officers and 10 Other Ranks laid in wait for Enemy Patrol in No Mans Land from 10pm to 1.30am but no enemy were observed.	
	29	9.	Nothing of importance happened. Our Snipers killed 2 of Enemy and a large file of enemy were observed on a trailing of 330 True from R.4.c.0.5.0.	

Army Form C. 2118.

WAR DIARY
or
INTELLIGENCE SUMMARY

(Erase heading not required.)

2/7 Sherwood Foresters

Place	Date	Hour	Summary of Events and Information	Remarks and references to Appendices
In the Field	June 30 1917		Got Patrol of 2 Officers and 18 Other Ranks with a Lewis gun waited in No Mans Land for enemy Patrol from 10pm to 1am. No enemy were seen or heard of. Enemy shelled our Front line with about 60 Rounds of 77 mm	

Holsworth
Major
Commanding 2/7 Sherwood Foresters

WAR DIARY
or
INTELLIGENCE SUMMARY

Army Form C. 2118.

2/7 Nott, Derby
Vol 6

July 1917

Place	Date	Hour	Summary of Events and Information	Remarks and references to Appendices
In the Field	July 1/1 39		Left Bouccamp sector of the line being relieved by 2/5 Sherwood Foresters	A.P.
	1-4th		The Battalion went into support at Gonycourt Wood U.22.c.9.3. (57c S.E)	A.P.
	8th		Working Parties were provided every night by the Battalion	A.P.
	9/31st		Left Gonycourt Wood on night of 8th & proceeded to Mesnil Ossol (57c SW)	A.P.
			The Battalion undergoing strict Divisional Training	A.P.
			The Battalion was transferred from III Corps to VIII Corps during its stay at Mesnil.	A.P.
	30th		Draft of 105 Other Ranks arrived from the Base	G.Y. 4 MB

Wellington ?
Commanding 2/7 Sherwood Foresters

Army Form C. 2118.

WAR DIARY
INTELLIGENCE SUMMARY
(Erase heading not required.)

2/7 Sherwood Foresters

August 1917

Place	Date	Hour	Summary of Events and Information	Remarks and references to Appendices
In the Field	Aug 1-31		Stationed at Le Mesnil. Engaged on Training.	
	24		Battalion moved by March Route to ALBERT.	
	31		Battalion moved by train to GODEWAERSVELDE and from there by march route to OUDEZEELE. Joined XIV Corps.	

G. Wellentyne Lt Col
Commanding 2/7 Sherwood Foresters

WAR DIARY or INTELLIGENCE SUMMARY

Army Form C. 2118.

59/178

Willwood Foresters
for month of SEPTEMBER 1917

Vol 8

Place	Date	Hour	Summary of Events and Information	Remarks and references to Appendices
	19th/20th		Battalion stationed at OUDEZEELE. Training continued with	
	20th		Battalion moved by march route to new area near POPERINGHE	
	20th/23rd		Battalion stationed at L13C area. Training continued with	
	23rd		Battalion moved to YPRES NORTH area by march route	
	24th		Battalion relieved 2/6th North Staffs in front line E of WIELTJE	
	25th		Battalion holding front line trenches.	
	26th		Battalion attacked on a two Company frontage as per orders attached. All objectives gained and maintained in spite of heavy enemy counter attacks. (See report of operations attached.)	40
	27th/28th		Battalion holding position captured on 26th.	
	29th		Battalion relieved by 2/6th South Staffs and moved back into support at SCHULER GALLERIES, POND GALLERIES and FORT HILL	
	30th		Battalion relieved from support line by one Company 2/5th CANTERBURY Regiment & marched back without incident to bivouacs at VLAMERTINGHE. Battalion resting. Casualties during the operations: Officers: Killed O/R 36 Killed, 138 Wounded, 48 Missing	

SECRET

OPERATION ORDERS BY LT COL N C MARTYN D C COMMANDING
2/7th SHERWOOD FORESTERS

Ref Map Sheet 28 N E 1/20000　　　　　　　　　　Copy No
Map attached　　　　　　　　　　　　　　　　　24th Sept 1917

(1) On ZERO Day at ZERO hour the 178th Infantry Brigade will attack the system of enemy trenches, Strong Points and Shell Holes etc between D.14, b.69, 99 and D.15 c 15, 90 and o.r present front line
　　The 177th Inf Bde will attack on the right and the 176th Inf Bde (89th Div) will attack on the left

(2) The Brigade will attack in two waves the areas, as per attached map, as under :-

　　1st Wave
　　　　On the right　2/6th S F will capture "R" Area
　　　　On the left　 2/7th S F will capture "S" Area

　　2nd Wave　right
　　　　On the laft　2/8th S F will capture "T" Area
　　　　On the left　2/8　 "   "   "   "U" "
These areas will be attacked and consolidated in depth

(3) The 2/7th S F will relieve the 2/6th N Staffs in the present front line of this Sector tonight, as under :-
　　Letter "D" Coy will relieve a portion of Letter "D" Coy 2/6th N Staffs in and so far as 1st and 2nd line exists
　　Letter "C" Coy will relieve remainder of Letter "D" Coy N Staffs and Shutes Galleries
　　Letter "A" Coy will relieve part of Letter "B" y 2/6th N Staffs in the "O" Area D 15 Central
　　Letter "B" Coy will relieve one platoon 2/6th N Staffs in Loos, with 1½ platoons, and one platoon in Pander Cat by 1½ Platoons
Guides for the relief will meet Coys at Dead End Corner at 9,30 pm
Companies will parade in their lines ready to move off at 6/0 pm under arrangements of C.Coys

(4) The Battn will take up, under cover of darkness the day night before ZERO Day, its positions of assembly
The following instructions for the assembly will be strictly observed :-

　　(a) There will be no movement in the area during daylight on the 25th

　　(b) At dusk before assembly O C Coys will proceed to previously reconnoitered positions and will mark out positions for assembly of platoons with discs and tape

　　(c) On completion of (b) platoons will be guided to positions of assembly for attack and assembly will be completed by 3 am

　　(d) Assembly Discs will be taken down and tape rolled up This will be completed by 4 am

(　(5) DISPOSITIONS OF ATTACK
　　　(a) The Battn will attack in two waves in depth
　　　(b) Compys will attack in the following order from the right :-

　　　"A" Coy　"D" Coy　 1st Wave
　　　"B" Coy　"C" Coy　 2nd wave

(c) The first wave will capture and consolidate "S" area as far as Green Line
The second wave will capture and consolidate "S" area between the Green Line and Red Line

(d) The boundary between Companies passes through D 13, a 99, 30 - D 13, 489, 45 - D 14, a 4 0, 49

(e) All strong points, fortified shell holes etc will be mopped up and occupied by the Compy responsible for the area

(f) Certain strong points exist in Battn Area (Cross Cottages - Fokker Farm - Green House, etc)
For the capture of these points O C Coys will detail special Platoons or Sections Likewise, should it be considered that these, after capture, should be held, garrisons for the purpose should be told off beforehand

(6) The Valley of the HANEBEEK will NOT be disregarded All positions on the South Bank will be accounted for by Companies on the left The 175th Brigade (58th Div) will account for all enemy positions N of the stream

(7) On night of 24/25 fighting patrols will be arranged for by 175th Inf Bde
Compy Commanders will send out "Ground Scouts" to thoroughly reconnoitre the ground to be fought over, and to act if necessary as guides to platoons

(8) BARRAGES

(a) A creeping Artillery Barrage will commence at ZERO hour 60 yards in front of forming up line and will proceed as under :-
To the Green Line 100 yards in 4 minutes
To the Red Line 100 yards in 6 minutes
After Red Line 100 yards in 8 minutes

The Artillery Barrage will pause as under :-
On the Green Line from plus 18 to plus 56
On the Red Line from plus 56 to plus 105
On the Blue Line from plus 145 to plus 185
On the Yellow Line from plus 205
The Artillery barrage will be H E with some smoke if possible

(b) A machine gun barrage from 40 guns organised in batteries will be placed on hostile strong points such as FOKKER FARM, TORONTO, OTTO FARM
It will lift from these points just before the Artillery barrage It will then fire on the HANEBEEK VALLEY and will subsequently lift to a general line BORDEAUX FARM BOSTHOEK - GRAVENSTAFEL

(c) If possible an Artillery smoke barrage will be placed along the HANEBEEK VALLEY from BORDEAUX FARM to RIVERSIDE

(9) The counter attack will be dealt with as under :-

(a) Artillery barrage fire called for by S O S Signal
(b) Machine Gun barrage fire called for by S O S
(c) Lewis Gun and Rifle Fire
(d) Direct machine gun fire from machine guns attached to the Battalion
(e) If necessary by supporting Battn, 2/5th N Staffs which will be pushed forward and will occupy the line "R" in DEEP TRENCH (C 14, d, 15, 75) - TORONTO

(10) MACHINE GUNS
One half section 178 M G Coy will co-operate with the Battn in the attack
In the attack this half section will not move forward until the last wave of the Battn has gone forward

(11) TRENCH MORTARS
Four guns will be in positions in or around WILTSHIRE GALLERIES in order to thicken up the Artillery barrage on CROSS COTTS and the neighbouring fortified shell holes. They will conform to lifts of Artillery barrage
On the capture of the above the guns some SOMELINE GALLERIES will go forward to positions at the above place for defensive purposes

(12) TANKS
Provided the weather is fine 1 Section Tanks will be employed to assist in the capture of OTTO FARM
They will also if possible available, render any assistance required when called upon. They will only be diverted from their objective under specially urgent circumstances. The signal for "TANK REQUIRED" is a sad helmet on rifle

(13) COMMUNICATIONS
O C Coys will be responsible for maintaining communications with troops on their flanks and also 2/8th Battn They will be prepared to render any assistance in the event of the unit on their flank being held up
The Signalling Officer (if not available the Signalling Sgt) will establish two forward stations. These should be as near the Company boundary as possible. He will select these positions immediately on going into the line and will inform Battn Headqrs of the positions selected

RUNNERS
Messages will only be sent by runners if Signals fail to maintain communication
Rally posts for runners will be established at ROAD HOUSE and CROSS COTTAGES
O C Coys will each detail three additional runners to report to Batn Headquarters at 3 pm on 25th inst. They will remain at Battn Headqrs and will remain on duty during operations
After ZERO HOUR all messages will be sent to Advanced Battn H Q

PIGEONS
Coys will each be supplied with pigeons for message carrying
These will be utilised only when all other means of communication have failed

CONTACT AEROPLANES
Contact Aeroplanes will assist during operations and will call for flares by succession of A's on Klaxon Horn
On this signal being given flares must be lit by advanced

(14) O C Coys are responsible for maintaining touch with the Battn on the left at their post at O ?, d 1, 4

(15) PRISONERS
Prisoners will be collected and sent back in charge of the smallest possible escort to Battn H Q where they will be handed over to the Provost Sgt
The latter will immediately send back the escort, if unwounded to O C Companies

(16) SYNCHRONISATION OF WATCHES
Watches will be synchronised at Battn H Q on the night before ZERO at 8 pm when one officer and one N C O from each Coy will attend

(17) DUMPS

Brigade Dumps have been established at WIND HOUSE and POND FARM
Battn Dumps will be notified later

(18) R A P

The R A P will be at POND FARM until one hour before dawn on
ZERO DAY when it will move forward to HINDUCOIT

O's C Coys will detail their Four reserve Stretcher Bearers to
report to the M O at HINDUCOIT at ZERO HOUR without their rifles and
equipment

Additional Stretcher Bearers will be supplied by Brigade and
these, together with the Regimental Stretcher Bearers, will be
responsible for the clearing of the Battle Front as far back as the
R A P

(19) Brigade Headquarters will be in TURTLE

Battalion Headquarters will be at CAPRICORN KEEP

Advanced Battn Headquarters will be established before ZERO HOUR
at SHULTZ GALLERY

IN THE FIELD
24 Sept 1917

F PRAGNELL
Capt & Adjt

Issued at 9 am by runner

Distribution - Normal
plus

(1) 174th Inf Bde Headquarters
(2) 2/5th S F
(3) 2/7th S F
(4) 2/8th S F
(5) 173th M G Coy
(6) 173th L T M B
(7) 173 Inf Bde (58th Div)
(8) War Diary
(9) File

ADMINISTRATIVE INSTRUCTIONS BY LT COL M G MARTYN M C
COMMANDING 2/7th SHERWOOD FORESTERS

(1) PICKS AND SHOVELS

The necessary picks and shovels will be drawn by Companies as under :-

"A" and "D" Coys will draw from Battn Mobilization Tools

"B" and "C" Coys will draw their tools at C 22, d,7,3, on their way up to the line to-night

When Coys come out of the line, as many tools as possible should be brought back

(2) LEWIS GUN LIMBERS

These will leave camp under Lt Parry at 5 pm and guides will meet them at Salvation Corner at 6 pm They will proceed to Spree Farm and their await arrival of Companies

Two men from each Coy will report to Lt Parry at 4.30 pm

(3) SANITATION

Strictest sanitary measures will be adopted in the line and after the advance has been made

(4) RATIONS AND WATER

All ranks must carry filled water bottles and no man is to be allowed to drink from the bottle or use it for any other purpose without orders from an Officer

A haversack ration will be carried as a supplement to the ration ordered under 59th Div Instructions for Offensive No 3

N C Os and men are to be warned to carefully conserve supply of water and rations carried, as these may be difficult to replenish

Captain Cooper will arrange for a supply of water in Petrol tins to be dumped at Battn Headquarters on the night of 25th inst

A tank for filling water bottles or Petrol Tins has been established on the ST JEAN - WIELTJE Road West of WIELTJE at C 28, b 25, 50

(5) RIFLES

Whilst in the line a rifle cleaning shop will be maintained at Battn H Q where a supply of six rifles will be maintained Men with rifles in bad condition and beyond cleaning in the line will hand them in and a clean rifle be given them at once

(6) BURIALS

Burials will take place at the following Cemetaries :-
WIELTJE C 28, a,7,5,
ST JEAN I 3, a,3,5,
BRIDGE HOUSE C 24, a,3,3,

If bodies are sent to any of the above places arrangements will be made to bury

(7) MACHINE GUNNERS

The Qmr will arrange with O C M G Coy with regard to rations for the half section attached to this Battn

These rations will be sent up with Battn rations

(8) TRENCH STORES

All trench stores will be taken over and handed over on relief, and receipt given

)9) CARRYING PARTIES

Carrying parties will be found by the Coys who will submit indents to Battn H Q for the stores, materials etc which they require sending up

Yukon Packs will be taken up the line by Coys.

(11) MARCH TO TRENCHES
During the march to the trenches distances of 100 yds will be maintained between platoons

IN THE FIELD
24 9 17

F PRAGNEL. L.
Capt & Adjt

ADDENDUM TO OPERATION ORDERS BY LT COL H C MARTYN M C
COMMANDING 2/7th SHERWOOD FORESTERS

(1) PRISONERS OF WAR
   Prisoners will be passed to the Divisional Cage by SPREE FARM - WIELTJE - ST JEAN route or by track No 4, 5 or 6 to Junction Road and thence to the Cage

(2) SEARCHING OF PRISONERS
   All prisoners will be searched immediately captured to ensure that they have no weapons concealed
   No personal effects such as decorations, watches, trinkets etc Identity Discs, Pay Books, Mess Tins, Water Bottles, Haversacks etc will be taken from prisoners, nor will they be searched for papers of tactical importance by the fighting troops, whose only duty in this connection will be to see that papers are not done away with by prisoners before they reach the Divisional Cage

(3) Escorts will take steps to ensure that prisoners do not converse with unauthorised persons

IN THE FIELD
24 9 17

F PRAGNELL
Capt & Adjt

SECRET

ADDENDUM NO 2 TO OPERATION ORDERS BY LT COL M C MARTYN M C COMMANDING 2/7TH SHERWOOD FORESTERS

The following are extracts from V Corps Artillery Instructions dated 23rd Sept :-

1. The "Creeping" barrage will be H E and Smoke on both Divisional fronts; the "Searching" barrage shrapnel only

   Shrapnel and not H E, will be used within 150 yards of either flank of the Corps

   No smoke will be fired from one hour after the final objective has been gained

   The protective barrage in front of final objective will continue at a steady rate for two hours, after which intermittent fire will be carried out A programme for this will be issued later

2. Two batteries of eighteen-pounders of the 65th Army Brigade R F A and one battery of 4.5" Howitzers belonging to the Artillery covering 59th Divl front, will, from zero until one hour after the final objective is gained, maintain a smoke barrage on the GRAFFENSTAFEL RIDGE between BOETLEER and ABRAHAM HEIGHTS

3. The attack will be preceeded by a two hours bombardment, which should not greatly exceed the bombardment of Sept 10th in intensity, in order that the enemy may suppose that it is the beginning of another 24 hours bombardment

   (a) This bombardment, as regards the Corps Heavy Artillery, will take the form of Crashes on areas which are likely to form serious obstacles to our advance and consolidation The MUHLE - ST JOSEPH(S INST: Ridge; ZONNEBEKE Village (between the BRICKYARD and the CHATEAU) ZONNEBEKE Station and WINDMILL HILL; DOCILE Trench and area about D.22, c.7,3, LEVI COTTAGES; VAN ISACKERE FARM; DOCHY FARM; OTTO FARM; and TORONTO FARM; should receive special attention

4. From the time of arrival on the final objective barrage lines, for a period of one hour and a quarter, and again from 2.15 pm till 3.30 pm and from 6 pm till 7.15 pm a gas barrage will be put down on likely assembly points and avenues of approach of hostile counter-attacks, provided the wind is safe

   Areas will be dealt with as follows :-

by 59th Division - D, 10, d,0,0, through BERLIN WOOD to WATERLOO FARM (D, 9, b,8,0)
Salvoes of H E should be occasibnally interspersed with the gas

5. For 24 hours after the capture of the final objective, the S O S barrage will be that detailed for the protective barrage When the S O S is received, all batteries will open fire at a rapid rate for 5 minutes, and at a reduced rate for 10 more minutes They will then cease fire, unless the call or signal is repeated

6. ACKNOWLEDGE

IN THE FIELD
24 9 18

F PRAGNELL
Capt & Adjt

ADDENDUM NO 3 TO OPERATION ORDERS BY LT COL M C MARTYN M C
                    COMMANDING 2/7th SHERWOOD FORESTERS

SECRET

1. Map "B" is cancelled and Map "C" substituted
    Map "C" Gives the stages of the attack and approximate times
of arrival and departure of Infantry at each stage
    It also includes the subdivision of areas the positions
of strong points to be constructed which are identical to those
in Map "B"

2 The attack will be immediately preceded by a bombardment
lasting two hours

3 The attack will be supported by the Field Artillery of 4
Divisions, and 8 Army Brigades also by 38 Siege and Heavy
Batteries

4 Cancel para 9 in previous Orders and substitute following :-
    Barrages The Field Artillery Barrage which will consist of
H E percussion and smoke shell will move as follows :-
    Open 150 yards from forming up line and lift at ZERO plus
3 minutes - thence for 200 yards at rate of 100 yards in 4
minutes - thence to Red line at rate of 100 yards in 6 minutes -
thence to final objective at rate of 100 yards in 6 minutes
  All lifts will be 50 yards

5 Para 9 in last Orders, last line should read D 1 4, d,15,75

6 The 21st Squadron R F C will detail a Contact Machine to be
over the objective at about :-
            ZERO plus one hour
            ZERO plus 1½ hours
            ZERO plus 2½ hours
and subsequently as ordered
The most advanced Infantry will light Red flares and signal
with Watson Fans when called for by KLAXON HORN or lights
The usual "counter-attack" aeroplanes will be continuously
in the air throughout the day from ZERO plus one hour till dusk
They will be used to draw the attention of the attacking Infantry
to any sign of an enemy counter-attack developing The procedure
will be as follows :-
  (a) Counter-attack Plane will sound one long blast on the
        KLAZON HORN
  (b) A smoke bomb will be discharged The bomb will burst
about 100 feet below the machine into a white parachute Flare
which descends slowly leaving a long trail of brown smoke about
one foot behind it
    The supply of these bombs is very limited so too much
reliance must not be placed on this method of communication
Counter-attack aeroplanes are without the markings of the Contact
Aeroplanes

7 Units of all sizes will establish and maintain communications with their flanks during the operations All leaders down
to Sections will meet their flank leaders prior to the attack,
and settle definite points as their respective boundary lines

8 Cancel para 16 of last Orders and substitute following :-

    Watches will be synchronised at Battn HQ on night before
ZERO at 10.30 pm when one officer and one NCO from each Company
will attend

9 Para 9 (a) of previous orders is cancelled Further instructions will be issued later

10. ZERO DAY ZERO HOUR will be notified later

11. ACKNOWLEDGE

IN THE FIELD
24 9 17

F PRAGNELL
Capt & Adjt

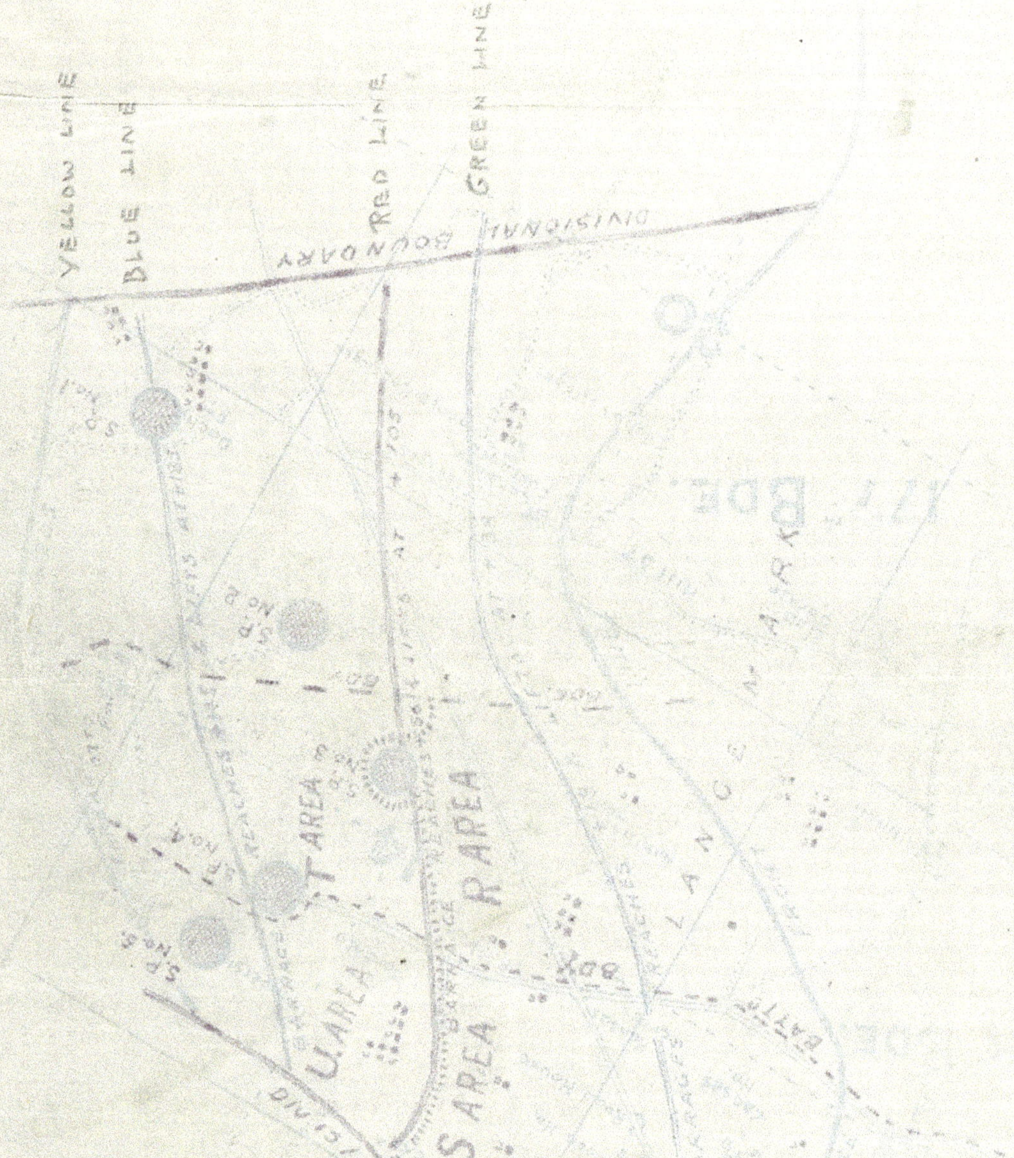

Addendum Notes to Operation
Orders by Lieut Col. McMartry [?]
commanding 2/7th Sherwood Foresters

1. Barrages. Barrages as views of addendum
No 3. Barrages will be as per
attached map. BIZARO + 178
protector barrage will move forward
at the rate of 100 yards in 8 minutes.
To beyond OTTO FARM when it
will dwell.

2. Contact Aeroplane. The distinguishing
mark on contact aeroplanes is
black flag on under of each aircraft
wing.

3. S.O.S. Signal. Men carrying S.O.S. Signals
will be distributed in each Pk by Companies.
If there is any fog S.O.S Signals when
sent up will be taken up by all
units as far back as Brigade H.Q.

Bouquell[?] [signature]

To Headquarters
　178th Infantry Brigade
　　　　　　REFERENCE YOUR 688/9

On the night of the 23/24th I received Operation Orders from G.O.C. 178th Infantry Brigade, giving details for the attack on the 26th

On the evening of the 24th the Battalion moved up and took over the line from the 6th North Staffs., the line running roughly SCHULER FARM SCHULER GALLERIES LOOS

On the morning of the 25th the enemy put down a heavy barrage on the front line and on the line CAPRICORN KEEP CORN HILL FORT HILL. This barrage lasted about 2½ hours.
A practice barrage was put down by our own guns at 6 pm and was replied to by the enemy by a barrage lasting about 2 hours, on the same lines as above. From observations made this practice barrage seemed very effective.

By 3.30 am on the morning of the 26th the Battalion formed up in 2 waves on 2 Company frontages on lines which had been previously taped under cover of darkness; In the front wave "D" Company on the left and "A" Company on the right, and the rear wave "C" Company on the left and "B" Company on the right.

During the night orders were received that ZERO hour would be 5.50.
At about 4 am a bombardment by our guns was put down on the enemy lines, which apparently proved effective. At this time an enemy barrage was put down on our rear waves, but caused few casualties
The Battalion advanced and the barrage was lifted according to time table

The first wave suffered a fairly number of casualties through Machine Guns at KANSAS HOUSE and the strong points round CROSS COTS.

The first objective was then consolidated by the first wave, the 2nd wave leapfrogging over, and here direction was slightly lost. A position about D.14. a.5.2. was captured by a Section of the right Company. It was then handed over to the Battalion on the right.
From here little opposition was met by the 2nd wave on to their 2nd objective, most of the casualties being through enemy shells. The 2nd objective was then captured and consolidated

I received a message at 7.15 am that the first objective was in our hands at 6.20 am
At about 7.30 am I received another message to say that we had captured and were consolidating the 2nd objective at 7.15 am

During the morning and early afternoon enemy shelling was not heavy on the front line, but was on the 2nd line and the rear area about SCHULER GALLERIES and CAPRICORN KEEP

About 2 pm the enemy launched a local counter attack which was broken up by our Artillery Fire. This barrage was apparently brought down by one of our Aeroplanes who spotted the enemy concentration.

About 5.30 the enemy put down a creeping barrage apparently on the whole of the front line, and he then launched a heavy counter attack. The troops on the extreme right and left flanks, for some reason unknown, then began to retire.
I am not clear as to whether there were any troops in my immediate front or not. None were seen.

An S O S Barrage was put down by our own Artillery, and also a heavy barrage by our barrage Machine Guns, both of which seemed to prove effective. In any case, the counter attack stopped before reaching our front line. The nearest enemy did not get to a point nearer than 450 yards. The enemy then shelled the region of our front line and KANSAS HOUSE. By this time stragglers had been collected and the front line reinforced, and the unit holding the 3rd objective were collected and sent up into their original position to reinforce a small body who had apparently still remained in their position

From about 9.30 pm there was practically no shelling whatever.

The usual barrage was put down by the enemy about 4 am on the morning of the 27th. During the day intermittent shelling of front line as far back as CAPRICON KEEP.
At 6 pm the enemy put down an intensive barrage on the areas POKKER FARM NILE KANSAS CROSS CROSS COTS SCHULER GALLERIES POND GALLERIES CAPRICON KEEP, which lasted until 8 pm. It is not clear on what portion of the line the enemy counter attack was launched. Considering the intensity of the barrage few casualties were suffered and the men shewed extra ordinary good morale in face of the heavy shelling After the barrage had ceased the night was quiet.

The usual shelling took place between 6 and 7 am on the 28th which was continued intermittently throughout the day.

About 6 pm S O S Signals went up on our flanks, which brought down very heavy shelling from the enemy guns. At 7 pm the shelling on both sides died down, and the Battalion was relieved by the 2/6th S. Staffs the relief being completed about one hour after it commenced
The Battalion was then withdrawn and split up into three parties, one to SCHULER GALLERIES, one to POND GALLERIES and one to FORT HULL.

On the 29th the usual intermittent shelling took place, and arrangements were made with the 2nd Battn Canterbury Regiment Anzacs for relief at night. The Battn was relieved by one Company of the 2nd Canterbury Regt, half an hour after the relief commenced.
The Battn then marched back to VLAMERTINGHE No 2 Area, via YPRES

IN THE FIELD
2 10 17

Lieut Col
Commanding 2/7th Sherwood Foresters

Army Form C. 2118.

2/7 Nott & Derby

Vol 9

WAR DIARY
or
INTELLIGENCE SUMMARY
(Erase heading not required.)

Place	Date	Hour	Summary of Events and Information	Remarks and references to Appendices
	4/9/17		Batt. moved by train from Hazebrouck to STEENBECQUE and marched to WITTES. Batt. engaged in reorganising & training.	ac
	5/9/17		Batt. moved by bus and marched to RECKLINGHEM. Training continued.	ac
	10/9/17		Batt. moved to HECHIN and ROUVAL. Half batt. at each place.	ac
	11/9/17		Batt. marched to PRESSY-LES-PERNES and BOURS. Half batt. at each place.	ac
	13/9/17		Batt. marched on and to GAUCHIN-LEGAL.	ac
	18/9/17		Batt. moved up to DIVISIONAL RESERVE and proceeded by march route to VANCOUVER CAMP (nr CHATEAU de la HAIE) Training continued.	ac
	19/9/17		Batt. proceeded by march route to SOUCHEZ CAMP. the ZOUAVE VALLEY. Batt. engaged chiefly in working parties up the lines.	ac
	24/9/17		Batt. moved up into Support in RED TRENCH. Map Reference 1. B.H.Q. S12 & 64. While in Support Batt. provided two of Wardle parties & CTs CYRIL and BEAVER by day and no working parties to forward areas by night. BALSAM/THE 2/5 sgts/16 Sherwood Foresters were in the line.	ac
	29/9/17		Batt. relieved 2/5 & Sherwood Foresters who returned to Support and in RED TRENCH. Batt. sector from N.33 d.45.25 to N.33 d. 1.2. Batt. HQ T.3.a.2.8. The 2/8 Sherwood Foresters were on our left. The 48th Division were doing a period of Division on our left. Situation on our line was normal. R.B. Buckworth, Maj. 2/7 Sherwood Foresters	ac 9.x

2/7 Notts & Derby
Vol 10

WAR DIARY
or
INTELLIGENCE SUMMARY.
(Erase heading not required.)

Army Form C. 2118.

Place	Date	Hour	Summary of Events and Information	Remarks and references to Appendices
	Nov 1		Batt" in front line Rest" H.Q. T.2.b.28 (Ref. 36.c. S.W.)	0C
	Nov 6		Batt" relieved by 2/4 South Staffords Batt" proceeded by light railway to VANCOUVER CAMP.	0C
CHATEAU DE LA HAIE.				
	Nov 6 to 14.		Bat" engaged on organizing working parties and training.	0C
	Nov 14		Bat" proceeded by march route to ETRUN.	0C
	Nov 15		Bat" stationed at ETRUN - engaged in training	0C
	Nov 19		Bat" proceeded by march route to No. 4 CAMP, HENDECOURT.	0C
	Nov 19 to 22		Bat" stationed at HENDECOURT - standing by to move at 2 hours notice.	0C
	Nov 24		Bat" proceeded by march route to GOMMIECOURT.	0C
	Nov 24		Batt" marched to BIHUCOURT and proceeded by tactical train to EQUANCOURT.	0C
	Nov 26		Bat" proceeded to VILLERS PLOUICH and was attached to 20th DIVISION for work on new line.	0C
			Batt" occupied trenches in R.14.D. (SHEET 57.c)	0C
	Nov 27		Batt" returned to EQUANCOURT.	0C
	Nov 29		Bat" proceeded by march route and occupied trenches in K.36.a v c. (Sheet 57.c)	0C
			The Bat" in DIVISIONAL RESERVE	0C
	Nov 30		Batt" moved forward and occupied trench in K.30.d (Sheet 57.c)	0C

10X

W. Shann Lt Col
Comdg 2/7 Sherwood Foresters

2/7 Nott/[Derby]
Army Form C. 2118.
December 1917. Sheet 1

WAR DIARY
INTELLIGENCE SUMMARY.
(Erase heading not required.)

Vol 11

Place	Date	Hour	Summary of Events and Information	Remarks and references to Appendices
	1/2		Battalion in Divisional Reserve at RIBÉCOURT	Ap.
	2		Battalion relieved 2/6 N. Staffs. In support to 1/7 Inf Bde. on line of Sunken road L12c0 L12e L12a+6 (57c)	Ap.
	3.4		Battalion holding support line as above	Ap.
	5		Battalion flew two Companies of Brunswicks forming outpost line along Sunken road from K6633 along Sunken road to L2L2B (57c) Brunswick front line evacuated – all troops passed through own line by 5am. Many artillery registered on outpost line. Small enemy patrols seen during day along line GRAINCOURT – ANNEAUX – CANTAING. At night own patrols came into contact with body of enemy at L2a17	Ap.
	6		Orders received at 2/30AM to form a defensive flank on the right of outpost line to conform with withdrawal of Divisions on right flank. New line of posts from L10.65 – L7.56 – L7d92 dug and occupied in dawn. Letter A Company and one Company of 2/4 Lines were withdrawn from outpost line to HINDENBURG Support line in K24a+b during this operation	Ap.

11-X

WAR DIARY
or
INTELLIGENCE SUMMARY.
(Erase heading not required.)

Army Form C. 2118.

Sheet 2

Place	Date	Hour	Summary of Events and Information	Remarks and references to Appendices
	6		Our patrols captured two prisoners at L.1.d.5.9 and one at K.6.b.9.5. Enemy Artillery shelled Sunken road in L.1.C. during morning. Small parties of enemy approached the right of our line during the morning but were driven off by rifle and L.G fire. 2/30 pm to 3/30 pm the enemy put down an intense barrage on outpost line and area L.7.c & L.13.a.+b. — this was followed by strong enemy attack along whole outpost line. At 3/50 pm outpost line ordered to withdraw to HINDENBURG SUPPORT line. Repeated S.O.S. was sent up but our Artillery barrage did not come down until 20 minutes after our S.O.S.	
6/6/10	10		Battalion in support in HINDENBURG SUPPORT line in K.24.a.4.6. Battalion relieved by 2/5 S.Staffs & proceeded to HINDENBURG line from K.35.a.3.4 to K.35.c.1.9.4. Battalion reported 178 Brigade.	
10.6.17	14		Battalion in reserve to 178 inf Bde in HINDENBURG line from K.35.a.3/4.to K.35.c.9.4. Battalion bivouacked to left owing to change of Divisional Boundary. Battalion relieved by 2/9 Bn. S.Ken. Regt. & proceeded by march route to BERTINCOURT	

Army Form C. 2118.

Sheet 3.

WAR DIARY
or
INTELLIGENCE SUMMARY
(Erase heading not required.)

Instructions regarding War Diaries and Intelligence Summaries are contained in F. S. Regs., Part II. and the Staff Manual respectively. Title Pages will be prepared in manuscript.

Place	Date	Hour	Summary of Events and Information	Remarks and references to Appendices
	19/5/22		Battalion reorganising + training at BERTINCOURT	J.P.
	22		Battalion proceeded by march route to Camp near ROCQUIGNY	J.P.
	23		Battalion proceeded by march route to B + C Camp. BEAUENCOURT.	J.P.
	25		Battalion proceeded by march route to BAPAUME, thence by train to PT. HOUVIN and thence by march route to GOUY-EN-TERNOIS	J.P.
	25 to 31		Battalion stationed at GOUY-EN-TERNOIS. Reorganising + training	J.P.
			Battle Casualties during month.	
			Officers.	
			Killed 2	
			Wounded 3	
			Other Ranks	
			Killed 12	
			Wounded 38	
			Missing 14	
			Wounded & M.I.	
				J.P. —

R.B. Rechyman Major
Comdg 2/7 Sherwood Foresters

WAR DIARY

INTELLIGENCE SUMMARY

2/6 North'd Fus.

January 1918

Army Form C. 2118.

Vol 12

Place	Date	Hour	Summary of Events and Information	Remarks and references to Appendices
	1918 Jan 1 to 31	30	Battalion stationed at Gouy-EN-TERNOIS and engaged in Training. 1st Line Battalion amalgamated with 2nd Line. R B Rickman Lieut Col Commanding 7th Kensington Fusiliers	F.1

12.X.

www.ingramcontent.com/pod-product-compliance
Lightning Source LLC
Chambersburg PA
CBHW081457160426
43193CB00013B/2515